ANCIENT MYTHOLOGY

ROMAN MYTHS AND LEGENDS

by Janie Havemeyer
illustrated by Cesar Samaniego

Tools for Parents & Teachers

Grasshopper Books enhance imagination and introduce the earliest readers to fun storylines and illustrations. The easy-to-read text supports early reading experiences with repetitive sentence patterns and sight words.

Before Reading
- Discuss the cover illustration. What do readers see?
- Look at the glossary together. Discuss the words.

During Reading
- "Walk" through the book with the reader. Discuss new or unfamiliar words. Sound them out together.
- Look at the illustrations. When and where does the story take place? What is happening in the story?

After Reading
- Prompt the child to think more. Ask: Which Roman myth or legend is your favorite? Why?

Grasshopper Books are published by Jump!
3500 American Blvd W, Suite 150
Bloomington, MN 55431
www.jumplibrary.com

Copyright © 2026 Jump! International copyright reserved in all countries. No part of this book may be reproduced in any form without written permission from the publisher.

Jump! is a division of FlutterBee Education Group.

Library of Congress Cataloging-in-Publication Data

Names: Havemeyer, Janie, author.
Samaniego, César, 1975- illustrator.
Title: Roman myths and legends / by Janie Havemeyer; illustrated by Cesar Samaniego.
Description: Minneapolis, MN: Jump!, Inc., [2026]
Series: Ancient mythology | Includes index.
Audience: Ages 7-10
Identifiers: LCCN 2024044362 (print)
LCCN 2024044363 (ebook)
ISBN 9798892137447 (hardcover)
ISBN 9798892137454 (paperback)
ISBN 9798892137461 (ebook)
Subjects: LCSH: Mythology, Roman–Juvenile literature. Gods, Roman–Juvenile literature. Goddesses, Roman–Juvenile literature.
Classification: LCC BL803 .H38 2026 (print)
LCC BL803 (ebook)
DDC 398.20937–dc23/eng/20241206
LC record available at https://lccn.loc.gov/2024044362
LC ebook record available at https://lccn.loc.gov/2024044363

Editor: Alyssa Sorenson
Direction and Layout: Anna Peterson
Illustrator: Cesar Samaniego
Content Consultant: David Potter, Francis W. Kelsey Collegiate Professor of Greek and Roman History, University of Michigan

Printed in the United States of America at Corporate Graphics in North Mankato, Minnesota

Table of Contents

Mighty Gods	4
Roman Gods and Goddesses	22
To Learn More	23
Glossary	24
Index	24

Mighty Gods

Ancient Romans believed gods and goddesses had powers. They could help or hurt people. Stories about them are known as Roman **mythology**.

Jupiter was king of the Roman gods. He was god of the sky. He could make it rain! His weapon was a thunderbolt.

Jupiter was not always king. His father, Saturn, ruled first. Saturn was a **Titan**. He did not want his children. He swallowed them!

Jupiter escaped. He gave Saturn a magic potion. It made Saturn throw up Jupiter's brothers and sisters. They fought Saturn and the Titans. They won! Jupiter made Saturn go far away. He locked other Titans in the **underworld**.

Jupiter became king. He also became god of the heavens. His brothers got important jobs, too. Neptune was god of the sea. Pluto became god of the underworld.

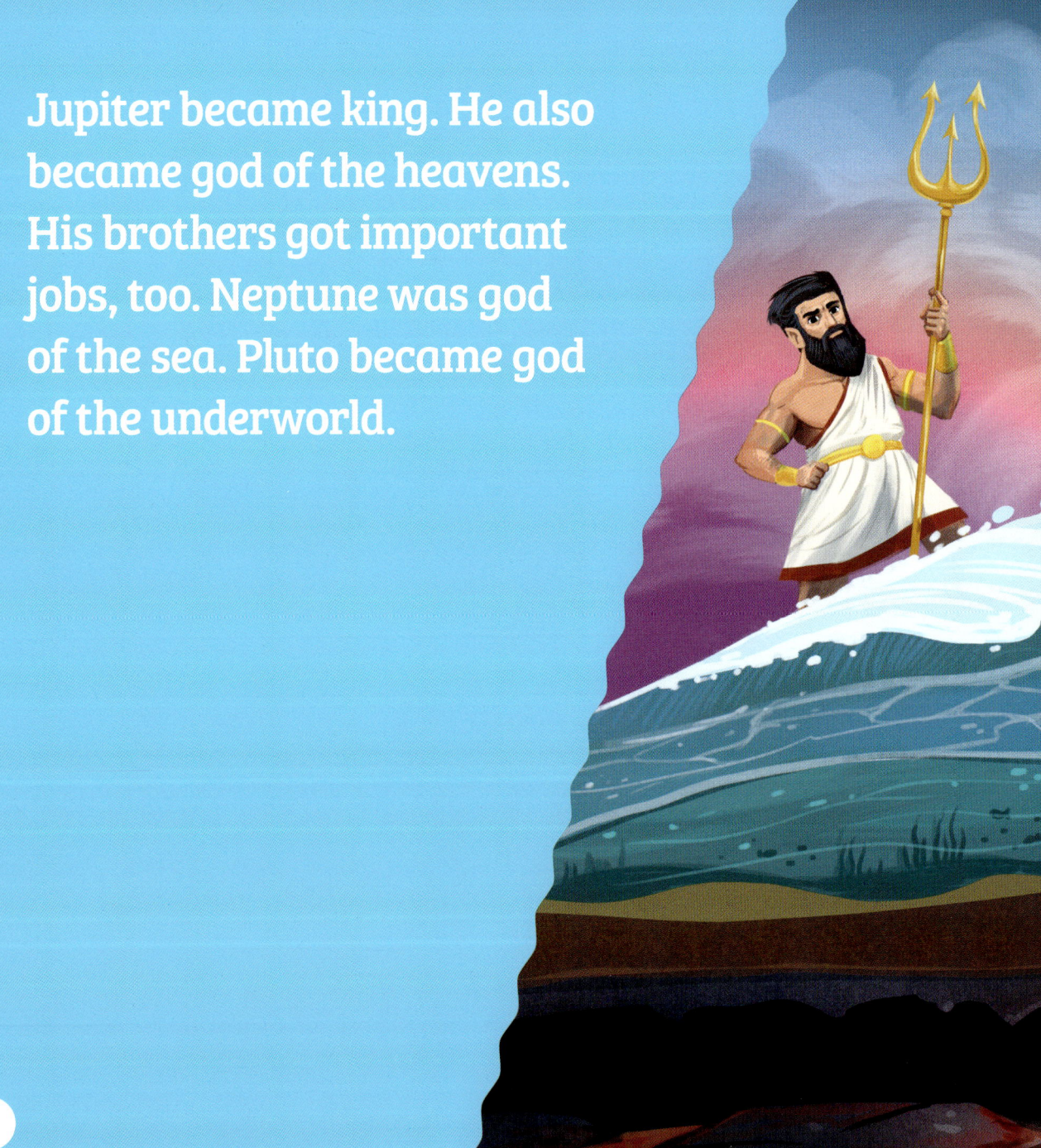

Minerva was one of Jupiter's daughters. She was the goddess of arts and war. One day, a woman named Arachne said she was better at weaving than Minerva. She challenged Minerva to a contest.

Arachne's **tapestry** was beautiful. But it made fun of the gods. Minerva was angry. She turned Arachne into a spider. Arachne spun webs for the rest of her life.

tapestry

Ceres was the goddess of **crops**. One day, her daughter Proserpina disappeared. Ceres searched all over. She was so upset that she did not help the crops grow. The land dried. Crops died. People went hungry.

Proserpina was in the underworld. She had married Pluto. Ceres wanted her to come home.

Proserpina stayed in the underworld for six months each year. Ceres was upset. Winter came. When Proserpina returned home, Ceres was happy. Spring came!

Hercules was one of Jupiter's sons. He was a brave hero, but a king made Hercules do dangerous things.

Once, he wanted Hercules to bring him Pluto's three-headed dog, Cerberus. Cerberus was strong. He guarded the gate to the underworld. Hercules wrestled him and won! He brought Cerberus to the king.

Mercury was the trickster god. One day, he and Jupiter pretended to be humans. They looked for food and somewhere to rest. They knocked on 1,000 doors. But no one would help them.

They came to a poor man's house. He and his wife fed the gods. The gods were happy. They turned the house into a beautiful **temple**. The man and his wife guarded the temple for the gods. It was an important job!

Mars was the god of war. He had twin sons named Romulus and Remus. When they were born, an evil king wanted them killed. The twins were put in a basket. They floated down a river. A wolf saved them.

When they grew up, the twins built a city along the river. The city became Rome. It is still in Italy today!

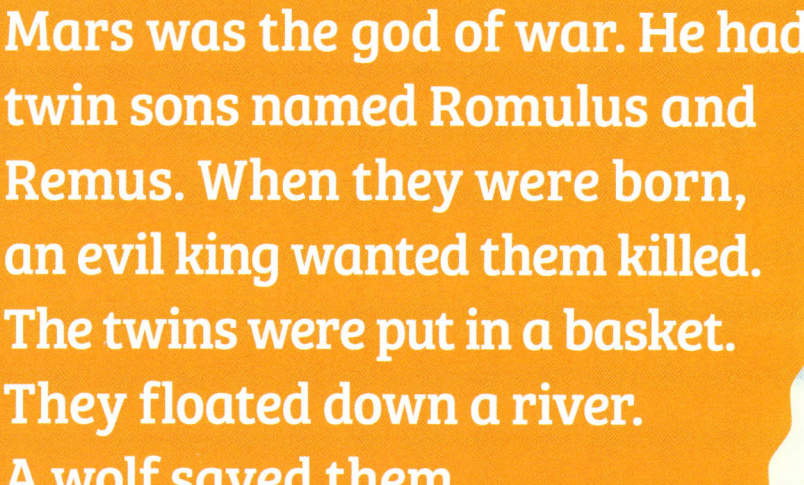

Roman Gods and Goddesses

Who are Roman mythology's most important gods and goddesses? Take a look!

Apollo
God of music, poetry, and healing

Ceres
Goddess of crops

Diana
Goddess of hunting and wild animals

Juno
Goddess of marriage and women. Jupiter's wife.

Jupiter
King of the gods. God of the sky and heavens.

Mars
God of war

Mercury
God of trickery, merchants, and travelers. Messenger for Jupiter.

Minerva
Goddess of arts and war

Neptune
God of the sea

Pluto
God of the underworld

Proserpina
Goddess of plants

Venus
Goddess of love and beauty

Vesta
Goddess of the home

Vulcan
God of fire

To Learn More

Finding more information is as easy as 1, 2, 3.

1. Go to www.factsurfer.com
2. Enter "**Romanmythsandlegends**" into the search box.
3. Choose your book to see a list of websites.

Glossary

ancient: Very old or from the very distant past.
crops: Plants grown for food.
mythology: A group of stories from a particular culture or religion.
tapestry: Cloth with threads woven into it to make pictures or patterns.
temple: A building in which a god is worshipped.
Titan: A giant who ruled Earth before the Roman gods.
underworld: A place in myths where the dead go.

Index

Arachne 10
Cerberus 16
Ceres 12, 14, 15
crops 12
Hercules 16
Jupiter 5, 6, 8, 10, 16, 18
Mars 20
Mercury 18
Minerva 10

Neptune 8
Pluto 8, 14, 16
Proserpina 12, 14, 15
Rome 20
Saturn 6
sea 8
thunderbolt 5
Titans 6
underworld 6, 8, 14, 15, 16